MW01611143

Your Child's

Road to Success

Begins at Home

Keysha Chester, M. Ed.

Your Child's Road to Success Begins at Home

ISBN# 978-0-9960611-0-0

Cover Design: Able Ramirez
Printed by 48HourBooks.com
Published by: Keysha Chester

For information, contact:
Keysha Chester
404-597-4645
ktchester1@gmail.com

Dedication

This book is dedicated to administrators, counselors, teachers, parents, and students. We are all on the same team. Let us all learn to work together.

One Team…One Goal…Profound Learning

Table of Contents

Acknowledgments

"For I know the plans I have for you," declares the Lord, "plans to prosper you and not to harm you, plans to give you hope and a future." Jeremiah 29:11

First and foremost, I would like to thank God. Thank you for listening, speaking, guiding, correcting, forgiving, and loving me.

I would also like to thank my loving parents and grandparents; my fantastic husband; my wonderful daughters; my amazing siblings, aunts, uncles, and cousins; and all of my friends and fellow educators.

Thank you for all of your support over the years.

A special thanks to Hotep and Hustle University for helping make my dream a reality.

Parent's Bill of Rights

1. You have the right to visit your child's classroom.
2. You have the right to see your child's school records.
3. You have the right to schedule a meeting with school officials as needed.
4. You have the right to see the tests your child has taken, given by his/her teacher.
5. You have the right to information for the electronic or paper version of your child's textbooks.
6. You have the right to view the teaching materials used in your child's school.
7. You have the right to attend school board meetings.
8. You have the right to request that your child be placed in a different class, depending on availability.
9. You have the right to request a different teacher for your child, depending on the availability.
10. You have the right to remove your child temporarily from a class or activity if you feel the activity is in violation of your religious or moral beliefs.

These are your rights. Please use them.

Parent Quiz

1. What is your child's best subject?

2. What is your child's hardest subject?

3. When was the last time you visited your child's classroom?

4. Do you volunteer at your child's school?

5. How many minutes a day does your child spend reading?

6. List your child's extra-curricular activities.

7. Do you attend school board meetings?

8. Does your child eat breakfast every day?

9. Does your child attend tutoring?

10. Rate your child's attendance on a scale of 1–10.

Home is the *first* school and parents are the *first* teachers.

<u>Preface</u>

You may be reading this book because your child has struggled with poor grades. Maybe you have been thinking of volunteering at the school but are not sure what you can do.

Well, you are not alone. Many parents struggle with the above issues, and many more.

This book was written to educate parents on how they can help their children be more successful in school. Are you ready? Believe it or not, your child's success in school begins at home.

The following suggestions and guidelines will help you make some small changes in your child's life that can bring about big results. Be encouraged.

You may already be doing many of the things on this book. That's great! If there are some things you aren't doing, it is never too late to change.

Let's get started!

Success

Begins

at

Home

Start the Day off Right

Breakfast is the most important meal of the day. Unfortunately, however, every day, the bell rings to start the school day with hungry students. Many parents may not realize that when their children don't eat breakfast it can make the day more difficult for the children and the teachers. Being hungry may cause your child's grades to suffer or cause your child to have unnecessary behavior issues. The good news is that there are a few things you can do to make sure your child is not like the ones discussed above.

Below are a few tips you can use to get your child's day started off on the right foot.

If you choose to provide breakfast at home, some easy breakfast items are a piece of fruit, toast, cereal and milk, or oatmeal. You want to make sure that the breakfast is nutritional as well as filling. If your child does not eat at home, then look into the school's breakfast program.

Some schools offer breakfast free to all students, regardless of parental income. How great is that! If the school breakfast is not free, it is typically cheaper than the school lunch. The food offered varies from cereal and milk to French toast sticks and sausage. Regardless of the menu item, it is important that your child starts the day off with a full belly.

At the beginning of every school year, parents are given the opportunity to submit applications for free or reduced breakfast and lunch. There are certain income requirements that have to be met. Make sure the application is completed and returned before the deadline. If you do not complete and turn in the application, you will be responsible for paying for breakfast and/or lunch.

FYI, there are a few additional benefits given to students who qualify for free/reduced lunch. For example, your child may qualify for reduced or waived fees for dual-credit classes and AP testing. Those small savings can help a lot.

If your family is having financial difficulties, please contact the guidance counselors and/or school administrators. They may be able to direct you to organizations that can offer your family some additional assistance.

School Supplies

A cook cannot prepare a great meal without the right utensils. A painter cannot create a masterpiece without the proper brushes. Well, students cannot do their greatest work without the necessary supplies as well. Students need pencils, pens, notebook paper, and folders every day.

It is very difficult for a teacher to get the class started or for your child to complete an assignment if he/she doesn't have a pencil and/or paper. The distraction continues further when kids try to borrow supplies from each other. All of this can be avoided by making sure your child is bringing the appropriate supplies to school every day.

Many government organizations, churches, and other organizations offer free school supplies. Check with the school and look for information on the TV, Internet, and the radio. In my area, we have school supply giveaways hosted by various counties. There is also a great organization called World Vision that offers free supplies such as paper, pens, pencils, and crayons to teachers so that they can give the supplies to students who need them or use them in class. Check with your child's school to see if they are aware of this program and if it is available in your area.

Also, keep your eye on the sales papers. Staples, Office Depot, Office Max, and other stores offer great discounts on certain school supplies. Don't forget about the dollar stores, such as Dollar Tree. I am a teacher and I get a lot of my supplies there. It's hard to beat a dollar!

By making sure that your child takes the necessary supplies to school daily, you are teaching him/her the importance of being prepared. This principle will carry over well in your child's future.

Again, if you are having financial difficulties, speak with your child's teacher and/or guidance counselor. The school might be able to help.

Attendance

Getting your child to school every day and on time may not always be easy, but it is very important. It teaches your children the important lessons of being on time. You may or may not realize it, but some school funding is attached to attendance. It is called the Average Daily Attendance, or the ADA. When a child is absent from school, skips school, or is tardy, it can potentially cause the school to lose money.

If your child takes the bus, he/she needs to arrive at the bus stop at least five minutes before the scheduled pickup time. If you drop your child off at school, make sure you have enough time to make it through the drop off line, time for your child to eat (if she/he eats at school), and for your child to make it to class before the bell rings to start school.

Also, verify your child's attendance to ensure sure he/she is not skipping school. If you receive an email or phone call from the school stating your child was absent or tardy, and you were not aware, you need to follow up to verify if the information is accurate. If the school has made a mistake make sure it gets corrected. If your child was skipping or tardy then you need to discuss the importance of being on time and present in class.

Schools and courts are beginning to give parents fines for their children's excessive absences or tardiness issues. What you don't know about your child's attendance can cost you.

When you make sure you get your child to school on time and stress the importance of attendance at an early age, it shows your child how important it is to be punctual. This is a skill your child will need for life.

Rest Up

Sleep… it does a body good. At the end of every day, try to make sure your child gets a good night's rest. Many children are sleeping or doing poorly in class because they don't have the energy to get their work done.

Younger children need at least 8–10 hours of sleep every night. Young children can become quite cranky when they are sleepy. As children get older, they don't require ten hours of sleep, but they do need at least about eight hours.

The mind has to relax before the body can relax. How can you help your children get a better night's rest? Consider cutting down on the TV time, Internet usage, and time on electronic devices about an hour or so before bedtime. As a family, try to work together to find different ways for your child to relax so that his/her mind is not going 100 miles per hour when it is time to go to bed.

Education is the passport of the future, for tomorrow belongs to those who prepare for it today.

~Malcolm X

Reflection and Planning

Grade yourself below:

Start Your Day off Right	A	B	C
School Supplies	A	B	C
Attendance	A	B	C
Rest Up	A	B	C

What are you doing that is great in these areas?

_____

_____

_____

What areas need improvement?

_____

_____

_____

What additional help or information do you need?

_____

_____

_____

New Parent Action Plan for Your Child's Road to Success:

_____

_____

_____

Homework and Extra Practice

Read, Read, Read

Children should be exposed to reading early. Learning to read at an early age will benefit your child for life.

A child's reading ability ties in with grades and testing scores in all subjects. If your child struggles with reading, then he/she may also struggle with math, science, and social studies. It's just that simple. Almost all subjects require some reading.

Why is reading every day important? Look at the following example. **Child A** reads five minutes a day and will end up reading about 282,000 words in a year. **Child B** reads 20 minutes a day and will end up reading about 1,800,000 words in a year. That is a huge gap, and the gap continues to grow every year. Over a ten-year period, **Child A** will have read 2,820,000 words, whereas **Child B** will have read 18,000,000 words! That's a huge difference.

How can you get started? Where can you get books for your child to read? The school library should have plenty of books your child can check out, or you can go to the public library. There are also book stores, eBooks, and used books you can purchase online or at a used book store.

How can you get your child to practice reading? You can read to your child, you can have your child read to you or a sibling, or your child can even listen to and read along with an audio book. Audio books can help children improve fluency and reading with expression. Also, as parents, we have to practice what we preach. Your children should see you reading as well.

Reading helps expose your child to new worlds, gives them more confidence when it is time to read in front of others, and teaches them lots of new things.

Reading is very important because we have to read all day every day, from the McDonald's signs to street signs. Reading is everywhere. Make reading a priority for your family.

Remember, in order for your child to become a better reader, he/she has to read, read, and then read some more.

<u>Practice Math (1 + 1 ≠ 3)</u>

I have taught quite a bit of math over the years, and I have come to notice that a lot of students today do not know their basic math facts. I have seen students in the 8th grade still counting with their fingers to solve 12 + 5. Is there anything that can be done? Yes, it's never too late.

What can be done? I am glad you asked. For starters, make sure your child practices and memorizes the basic math facts early. There comes a time, hopefully in elementary school, when your child learns the basic facts of addition, subtraction, multiplication, and division. If you have your child to practice with flash cards and do speed drills he/she will have their facts memorized in no time.

More and more states are giving timed tests, many of which are about speed and accuracy. Unfortunately, many students turn in exams with unanswered questions because they had to spend so much time focusing on calculation.

Memorizing math facts has many benefits:
- helps with estimation problems.
- helps children learn to count money and make sure they get/give the proper change.
- is the foundation for all future math courses.
- reduces dependence on a calculator.

Basic math is the foundation of advanced math. If the foundation is weak then future math classes will be very difficult.

Make Homework a Priority

Homework provides an opportunity for your child to get more time to practice what he/she learned during the day. It is very difficult for many children to grasp new lessons by only practicing in the classroom. Teachers assign homework to give kids another opportunity to master what they have been working on in class.

Many schools coordinate homework nights. For example, the teachers might decide to give only math homework on Monday and Wednesday, English on Tuesday, science on Thursday, and history on Friday. Having this type of schedule can help you to know what your child should be working on every night. It also cuts down on too much homework per night and allows children to have time to participate in extracurricular activities.

If your child's school does not have something like this set up, you may want to make the recommendation. If you can think of any other ideas, please share them with your child's teacher or the school administrators. Schools do not have all the answers; they want and need your help.

Here are a few more suggestions:
• When your child comes home from school, let him/her have a break or nap before starting on homework.
• Give him/her an after school snack.
• Turn off the TV and other electronic devices.
• Check the school website or your child's agenda to make sure she/he is doing the right assignment. Knowing what the assignment is gives you an idea of how long it should take to complete the assignment. For example, if your child only has five short math questions, it should not take two hours to complete.
• Have a dedicated time and place set up in the house

for your child to work on homework. You can let your child pick where he/she feels the most comfortable working. The kitchen table might be a good spot so that you can be available to answer questions while you prepare dinner. Allowing your child to work where he/she feels the most comfortable may help him/her child put more effort into the assignment.

• Help your child understand the importance of completing homework. Remember, school is his/her job; that's why teachers give classwork to do in class and homework to do at home. School is work.

• Make sure you know what is being taught every week, just in case the work is confusing for you. If you don't understand what your child is learning, you should talk to the teacher in advance and see if he/she has additional resources to help you. You should also check with friends and family to see if they can help.

• Look for examples on the Internet. Many topics covered in school have YouTube videos with teachers explaining the work or websites with sample problems.

• Check your child's homework to see if it is correct and make sure it gets put in his/her backpack so it can be turned in on time.

I Don't Have Homework

How many times have you heard your child say, "I don't have any homework?" Well, sometimes that's true. But, if that is your problem, here is the solution.

Students can always get additional practice or work on getting ahead. Your child's teachers may have some additional practice assignments or educational websites to recommend for your child. There are hundreds, if not thousands, of free educational websites. Extra practice is only a Google search away!

Students can always benefit from additional reading, practicing math facts, and test preparation.

An idle mind is not good. You should always have some educational tools in your toolbox for whenever your child gets bored. Your child won't be bored long.

Reflection and Planning

Grade yourself below:

Read, Read, Read	A	B	C
Practice Math	A	B	C
Make Homework a Priority	A	B	C
I Don't Have Homework	A	B	C

What are you doing that is great in these areas?

_____

_____

_____

What areas need improvement?

_____

_____

_____

What additional help or information do you need?

_____

_____

_____

New Parent Action Plan for Your Child's Road to Success:

_____

_____

_____

Grades

and

Activities

School and Classroom Websites

Schools and teachers are able to use more technology than ever before to make the connection between school and home. Many teachers use a website like www.classjump.com. This site allows teachers to share the class syllabus, which typically includes the teacher's planning period, class rules, tutoring schedule, textbook, and teacher contact information. The site also allows teachers to post class notes, assignments, dates for quizzes/tests, and general announcements. Parents can create an account so they can receive email notifications when the teacher's site is updated with new information.

Some schools have their own websites for teachers to use. Make sure you get the teacher's website address and add it as a favorite on your web browser for easy access.

You should be able to follow along with what your child is learning in class. Teachers typically have their lesson plans completed and posted before the new week begins. If the teacher does not have a website, you can still ask what the students will be learning so you can provide extra help and practice at home.

If you do not have Internet access at home, you can always go to the public library; many restaurants and stores have free Wi-Fi as well. You could also ask to use a family member's or friend's computer or ask them to check the website for you and keep you posted.

<u>Tutoring</u>

There may be times throughout your child's school years that he/she may need some additional assistance in a smaller setting. Tutoring may be the solution.

Most teachers offer **_FREE_** tutoring before and/or after school. Many districts do not provide transportation for tutoring and leave that responsibility with the parents. If that is the case, and your child needs extra tutoring, try to make the appropriate transportation arrangements so he/she can get the needed help.

If you are not able to drive your child to and from tutoring, you might want to try to make friends with other parents and you can work out a carpooling system together. You might also consider recruiting family members or friends to help.

If you can't make transportation arrangements or you would prefer to have someone else tutor your child, you can look for a tutor that can travel to your home. There are also many businesses that have a store front and will tutor your child for a fee.

Whether using school tutoring or hiring a tutor, do whatever you can to get your child additional help if he/she needs it.

Extracurricular Activities

Extracurricular activities are activities that children can participate in for fun and/or enrichment and can also lead to scholarships. Can you say *FREE MONEY*? Some additional benefits are listed below.

Sports – There are many benefits to children being involved in sports. A big benefit is that it helps children stay active and get exercise. Many children today are not very active, which can contribute to childhood obesity and other health problems.

Through sports, your child will also learn how to work with others. The skills he/she will learn regarding teamwork will help with group assignments in the classroom.

Schools have a no pass/no play system, and children have to keep their grades up in order to be able to play in the game. A lot of athletes keep their grades up in order to play and to avoid getting into trouble with their coaches.

If you would like to learn more about how playing sports can help your child, you can visit the U.S. Department of Health and Human Services website.

Clubs – There are great clubs for students to participate in that allow them to learn more about future careers or to volunteer and work in the community.

Participation in clubs can be added to college applications and helps to show how well-rounded your child is.

If there is a club that you think the kids at the school would like that's not available, and you can volunteer your time, schedule a meeting to speak with one of the school administrators to see if and how you can get it started.

<u>Fine Arts</u> – Many children have a desire to learn how to or are gifted in playing an instrument, singing, dancing, or drawing. Most schools offer some type of general music, choir, and art classes, starting in elementary school.

Middle and high schools typically have specific classes where your child can join the band, sing in the choir, take an art class, and some schools have a dance class as well. Students are given the opportunity to perform or showcase their talents within the school and can compete in events outside of the school as well.

Participating in extracurricular activities gives children the opportunity to travel to different places, overcome shyness, show off their talents, meet new people, and so much more. Many of these extracurricular activities can also lead to scholarship opportunities.

Make sure you and your family show up to support your child when he/she participates in extracurricular activities. Kids love that kind of stuff.

Progress Reports and Report Cards

Progress reports and report cards are issued by the schools to give parents feedback in regards to how their children are doing in school. The dates for progress reports and report cards are typically highlighted on the school calendar. Please make sure you are monitoring your child's work and grades regularly. Many parents are shocked to see their child has a failing grade, only to find out the child hasn't been turning in his/her work.

Progress reports are issued at the halfway point in the marking period, about every 3–5 weeks to let you know how your child is doing in class. These reports are printed and sent home or available for you to see online. Also, since they are issued at the halfway point, before the report card, you have time to get your child some tutoring, complete assignments, ask about extra credit, schedule a class visit, and/or schedule a parent–teacher conference.

Many schools have a website where you can check grades on a daily basis. This allows you to know how your child is doing even before the progress report comes out and before the problem gets too big.

Report card grades are very important. These grades will help to determine if your child is retained in the same grade for another year or promoted. Stay informed and work with your child's teacher to help your child be successful.

Review Schoolwork

When I was in elementary school, I had a friend whose mother would make her correct all of her wrong answers on the work she brought home. As a kid, that didn't make much sense to me, but as a parent it makes perfect sense.

Firstly, if your child has answered questions incorrectly, that indicates that he/she does not understand some concepts that should have been covered in class. This gives you a chance to sit with your child and work on those skills. The missed answers are examples of the type of tasks your child can work on with the teacher if your child goes to tutoring (or with the tutor if you hire one) or what you can help with at home.

Secondly, people make mistakes. I am a teacher, and yes, I admit we make mistakes. Going over the work gives you an opportunity to see if the paper has been graded correctly. If you feel you have found a mistake, contact the teacher to verify whether you are correct. If you find a mistake, and it is big enough to bring to the teacher's attention, then respectfully let the teacher know.

Thirdly, checking your child's work allows you to see if your child is really having difficulty in a subject and/or is in danger of failing a grade. By actively monitoring your child's progress and getting him/her the help needed you will reduce the chances for surprises on the report card.

Reflection and Planning

Grade yourself below:

School/Classroom Websites	A	B	C
Tutoring	A	B	C
Extra-Curricular	A	B	C
Progress Reports /Report Cards	A	B	C
Review Schoolwork	A	B	C

What are you doing that is great in these areas?

_____

_____

_____

What areas need improvement?

_____

_____

_____

What additional help or information do you need?

_____

_____

_____

New Parent Action Plan for Your Child's Road to Success:

_____

_____

_____

Family Matters, Special Needs, and Goals

Be Your Child's Biggest Cheerleader

When was the last time you told your child he/she was doing a good job? School can be hard for many children and some positive words might make a big difference. It is their job, and school requires a lot of work. Everyone loves to be praised and encouraged from time to time, including your child. Make it a practice to give your child positive feedback for doing a good job or showing improvement.

Many times, as parents, we don't take the time to tell our kids how great they are or that we see how hard they are working. We have to remember to reward and encourage desired behaviors as it will increase the odds of them doing it again.

Rewards or encouragement can come in different forms. Take your time to get know and/or ask your child what helps him/her to feel good about him or herself.

Some students may struggle academically. Not all kids are gifted in the same way. Make sure you find reasons to praise your child. All praise should be for something valid and appropriate. Do you have a child who struggles with turning in homework? Well, when your child does turn it in, make sure to say something positive to increase the chances he/she will do it again. Did he/she bring up a grade in a class? How about a small reward for showing you recognize the hard work it took to pull the grade up?

If your child is struggling, try to spend more time brainstorming solutions instead of fussing about the issue. Fussing doesn't really help anyone.

Take Some Parenting Classes

Were you born knowing how to drive? How about converting fractions? These topics pale in comparison to parenting. Children did not come with a manual and parenting is hard work.

My daughters had to take a six-hour online class before they could take the test to get their driving permits. They actually had to pass the test before they could drive. As hard as it is to be a parent, shouldn't you consider taking a class or two?

Parenting classes can help you deal with problems your child may be having with academics or behavior, and they can provide you with additional help if you have a special needs child.

Taking classes will also show your child that you are a life-long learner and that you value education by taking classes yourself. Plus, I don't care how old your child is, you can always learn something about parenting.

Suggested workshops topics:
- Better family relationships
- Helpful ways to deal with behavior problems at home and in school
- Parenting special needs children
- State test preparation
- District/school policies
- Training for volunteering in the school
- Understanding educational standards

Family Matters and Guidance Counselors

Circumstances are constantly changing in the lives of families. It is possible that there is a sick relative, divorce, marriage, or the death of a close family member or friend. All of these circumstances, and so much more, can have an impact on a child.

If your child seems to be struggling, talk with the teacher and/or guidance counselor to make sure your child is receiving all of the support he/she needs. Your child has a team of adults who should be working together to ensure his/her success. If you are beginning to notice problems at home with academics or behavior that may spill over into the school, please let the school know. Also, if you are concerned about grades, please talk to the teacher sooner rather than later. If you wait until the last minute, your child might fail that marking period. Your child may find comfort and needs to know that all of the adults in his/her life are working together.

Please make sure the school is aware of any issues that might be upsetting your child. Many times, kids are sad or crying in class, and that is when the school learns that something is going on at home. The school is there to help with your child's emotional needs as well as his/her academic ones, but they can only help if you let them know what is going on.

If you see changes in your child's behavior and you are not sure what is going on, you can still go to the school so you can work together to figure it out. Sudden changes in behavior, attitude, grades, or friends can be an indication of a bigger problem. Be proactive.

Below is a sample list of some possible situations that may cause changes in your child's behavior and warrant you alerting the guidance counselors.

- Births or adoptions
- Illness or death
- Physical, sexual, drug, or verbal abuse
- Suicidal thoughts
- Divorce
- Marriage
- Family relocating
- Behavior issues
- Drop in grades

Special Needs

All children are born with strengths and weaknesses, and many children might need some additional help in order to be successful. As a parent, you should be aware that there are additional resources available if your child has special needs.

There are processes, classes, and programs to help special needs students. The child's needs may be emotional, physical, or academic. Should you or your child's teacher have any concerns, it is possible that your child may need to be tested.

You are your child's biggest advocate; make sure that he/she is getting the help needed. Talk to the teachers, counselors, and/or diagnostician if you have any questions or concerns about your child and his/her special needs. Be sure to work with the school to ensure your child is receiving the appropriate assistance and make sure to attend all meetings.

There are also many organizations around the country to help parents of special needs children. If you or your child needs help, get it.

S.M.A.R.T. Goal Setting

Goal setting is a skill that can and should be used in many areas of a person's life. There are many types of goals. Some examples of goals your child can set are academic, financial, and social. One way of setting goals is to make sure that they are **S.M.A.R.T.**

Specific

Measureable

Attainable

Realistic

Timely

Let's start with the **S** for specific. Sometimes people set goals that are very vague. What if your child says, "I want to make better grades"? What does that really mean? How will your child know if he/she ever reaches his/her goal? A better goal might be to get a B in reading on the next report card.

Next, we have the **M** for measureable. A measureable goal should be able to show growth. Setting a goal to lose ten pounds is measurable, whereas a goal just to lose weight is not. Having a measureable goal helps to track the progress made toward accomplishing the goal.

A is for attainable. An attainable goal is one that actually can be accomplished. A goal of going from a 35 average in science to a 95 average in a week is typically not going to be attainable. If a goal is not attainable, the person is only setting him/herself up for failure and disappointment.

Then there is for **R** for realistic. The questions that have to be answered are whether or not the child is willing and able to do what must be done to accomplish this goal. If a child is not willing or does not have the ability to do what is necessary to accomplish the goal, then it will never happen. For example, is the child willing and/or able to get in the extra study time to bring up a grade? If the answer is that the child is not willing to or will not be able to because of other commitments, then it is not realistic to believe the goal will be reached.

Lastly, a goal must be **T**, or timely. An example of an untimely goal is to set a goal of three hours to answer ten simple math word problems. A better goal would be about 5–15 minutes to complete the task. The goal may or may not be accomplished in that time, but it gives your child something to shoot for. If your child doesn't reach the goal, he/she should have been close; give your child a little more time to finish. Then, the next time you set goals, consider adding a little more time.

Accomplishing goals requires planning. You will need to decide on a plan of action and consider the obstacles that might get in the way. By planning for success and figuring out how to overcome potential obstacles, you and your child will increase the odds of completing the goal.

P. S.

You may want to consider setting some goals for yourself and modeling the process, struggles, rewards, and satisfaction associated with accomplishing some of your own goals.

Reflection and Planning

Grade yourself below:

Be Your Child's Cheerleader	A	B	C
Parenting Classes	A	B	C
Family Matters/Guidance	A	B	C
Special Needs	A	B	C
S.M.A.R.T. Goal Setting	A	B	C

What are you doing that is great in these areas?

_____

_____

_____

What areas need improvement?

_____

_____

_____

What additional help or information do you need?

_____

_____

_____

New Parent Action Plan for Your Child's Road to Success:

_____

_____

_____

School Visits and Volunteering

Attend School Functions

Throughout the school year, parents are invited to attend various events that are designed to give parents and teachers opportunities to interact outside of the classroom. As much as possible, you should try to attend as many of these events as you can. The most popular events are open house, meet the teacher night, and parent–teacher conferences.

Open houses give you a chance to check out the school. Schools open their doors for parents to visit the school, get information, and ask questions. You can check out the library, tour the school, and get a feel for the whole campus. Open houses typically take place at the beginning of the school year. This is not the time to talk to the teachers about your child specifically. This meeting is to get general information about the school, classes offered, and some school procedures.

Meet the teacher night also takes place at the beginning of the year. By the evening of meet the teacher night, you should have your child's schedule. You can go around and check out the classrooms, introduce yourself, and find out information regarding specific class requirements. There will be lots of parents there to meet the teacher, and the teacher will be talking about the class in general. Some of the information you might get at meet the teacher night are the school supply list, classroom rules, and the academic calendar.

The parent teacher conference is when you get one-on-one time with the teacher to discuss your child. Parent teacher conferences are scheduled. Teachers typically have a planning period every day or every other day, so they schedule the conferences for those times. Conferences can be scheduled to be in person or over the phone. During this meeting, you can discuss your child's behavior and grades, see samples of the classwork, and get answers to any questions you may have. The parent teacher conference can be set up with one teacher at a time or with all of your child's teachers. You and the school should work together to come up with a time that is convenient for all of you. Depending on the purpose of the meeting, it might be a good idea to have your child attend so that he/she can hear what is said and answer any questions.

There are several benefits to attending these events. For one thing, it helps you get a feel for the school and the staff. Does the school feel welcoming? Another benefit is that it helps you and the teacher put a face to a name and to start building a relationship. Third, it shows that you are an active parent and that you care about your child's education and future.

Lastly, attend school board meetings. These meetings are generally held once a month. If you are not able to attend, many districts record the meetings and/or post the minutes. The school board members make the big decisions for your school district. Stay involved and informed.

It may not be possible for you to attend all of these events, and that's understandable. If you are unable to attend, try to get a family member, friend, or another parent to go to represent you.

Classroom Visits

Try to visit your child's classroom at least once a year. I am a teacher and a parent and I normally take a day off at least once a year to spend the day in my child's classrooms. It is probably best to start doing this when your children are younger, so they will already expect it when they get older. These visits should not stop at the elementary level. I visited classrooms when my daughters were in high school.

Educate yourself on the proper procedures for classroom visits. Each district has its own policies. For example, many schools like the parents to schedule their visits in advance. If you don't schedule your visit, they may not allow you to visit the classroom. There is no need to miss time from your job or take time out of your day to visit the school and not be able to accomplish your goal. Scheduling your visit can also allow your time in the classroom to be more productive. You don't want to take time off just to watch children sit quietly and take a test.

Here are some things you should look for when you make your classroom visit. Are the students engaged? How does the teacher deal with behavior issues? How was your child's behavior? Did your child get his/her work done? Did the students participate? Does your child feel the teacher was the same as when you are not visiting the classroom? Is the teacher teaching the educational standards for that class?

Since you are already at the school, you may want to take time to eat lunch with your child and his/her friends. This will give you an opportunity to get to know your child's friends, as well as to observe the school environment. Remember, you are in the classroom to quietly observe. Please don't disturb your child, other students, or the teacher.

If, after your visit, you have any concerns or questions, you should contact the teacher to schedule a parent teacher conference or meet with the principal. The teacher is not available to discuss issues with you during instructional time.

Conflict Resolution

Sometimes it is better to address a small issue before it becomes a big issue. Teachers, parents, and students are all human. Conflict is bound to arise. How should you handle conflicts with the school?

Please, please, please, please, please try to solve all issues at the lowest level possible. When issues arise in the classroom, if possible, try to work with the teacher to resolve the issue. If the teacher can't help, refuses to help, or doesn't know what to do, then go to the principal. Many times issues can be handled with the teacher. As a parent, you and the teacher should be on the same team; try to work together to come up with a solution.

Again, if the teacher can't or refuses to work with you, then you should go to his/her supervisor to discuss the issue. If the supervisor is not helpful, then talk to that person's supervisor, and so on. Always start small and work your way up.

Volunteer

Schools want and need your suggestions, support, and time. But how can you get involved?

You can join the Parent Teacher Association, or PTA. This will give you an opportunity to be an advocate for your child and the school. PTAs also raise funds and the extra money can go to pay for more technology, field trips, have guest speakers, or pay for fun activities. When run properly, PTAs allow parents and the school to work together to benefit the whole campus.

You can also be a chaperone for field trips and dances. The school always needs an extra adult set of eyes and hands. Most school districts require some form of background check. If, for whatever reason you cannot volunteer, try to get a family member or friend to work at the school. Aim to have at least one member of your family available to assist on various occasions.

Every year, schools have committees that make major decisions about staffing, budgets, and many other important issues. You can and should try to be a part of those committees. How much money does your school have in its budget? How is the money being spent? Who is going to be the next principal? Those are all big questions, and most parents receive the answers after the fact. The decisions being made in the school have a direct and indirect impact on you and your child. Get involved.

Reflection and Planning

Grade yourself below:

Attending School Functions	A	B	C
Classroom Visits	A	B	C
Conflict Resolution	A	B	C
Volunteering	A	B	C

What are you doing that is great in these areas?

_____

_____

_____

What areas need improvement?

_____

_____

_____

What additional help or information do you need?

_____

_____

_____

New Parent Action Plan for Your Child's Road to Success:

_____

_____

_____

Student Behavior, State Testing, etc.

Code of Conduct

In society, we need rules. We can't function without them, and schools are no different. Schools have to have polices for expected student behavior. The code of conduct is the written set of policies and procedures for the school and the district and should apply to all students.

Parents must educate themselves about these policies. Times have changed since you were in school, so do not assume that the rules are the same. Schools have rules regarding dress, tattoos, and piercings, just to name a few. Take time to educate yourself about them.

After you have read over the code of conduct, you might find that you have some questions. If so, get your questions answered sooner rather than later. There can be serious consequences for violating these rules, and saying that you or your child didn't know or understand the rules won't make much difference. Even if you or your child did not know his/her actions were against the rules, your not knowing will not keep your child from being punished.

You may also find that you disagree with some of the rules and/or consequences. In that situation, you have limited options. You can talk to the school administrators and/or school board about your concerns to see if the rules can be changed. Other options are to relocate your child to another school or consider homeschooling.

Behavior in School vs. Out of School

Have you ever been to a football game? Can't you just see all the fans yelling, screaming, and having a good time? How about the library? It is very quiet, and if anyone is communicating, they are usually whispering.

The previous examples are to demonstrate that where you are dictates how you should behave. Learning how to behave in different environments is a skill you must teach your child.

The school and classrooms are very structured environments. Teachers only have about 45 minutes per subject to educate their students. That really is not a lot of time. Every second a child is off task hurts that child, the other children, and the teacher.

What are some behaviors you should talk to your child about?

- Have school supplies.
- Follow instructions the 1st time they are given.
- Be silent during instruction and classwork unless the teacher says otherwise.
- Be respectful.
- Keep electronic devices put away.
- Try to go the restroom before school, during passing periods, at lunch, or after school.

- Only work on the assignment given by the teacher.
- Stay awake in class and maintain an inside voice.
- Pay attention, ask questions, and participate.
- Ask for permission to get up.
- Wait to be called on to answer a question.
- Don't argue with the teacher. If your child has a problem with the teacher he/she should tell you and let the adults handle it.

Emergency Contact

Emergencies happen every day. Please make sure that you have the accurate school information in case you need to contact them, and that the school has your accurate information in case they need to contact you or a family member.

State Testing

Each year, teachers are tasked with educating your child with specific knowledge and skills, or educational standards. In the majority of the United States these standards are called the Common Core, and in Texas they are called Texas Essential Knowledge and Skills (TEKS). The educational standards are the basis for what the teacher teaches, what students should learn, and the questions on the high-stakes exams that your child has to take and pass almost every year.

State testing is a huge issue in education across the United States. Children are drilled and tested all year in preparation for the big one. Scores from the state exam determine whether students will be promoted or held back for the next school year. The scores also determine how well the school is doing as a whole, and believe it or not, who gets hired and fired.

As important as state testing is, as a parent, you should learn as much as you can about it. How? Visit your state's department of education website to learn what the standards are for the grade level your child is in. Also, see if there is a copy of a released test on your state's department of education website, or ask a teacher at your child's school. If they do not have actual questions from a released test, they should have some examples of what the questions look like.

Use the information to help your child to prepare, as the consequences for failure are very high.

Begin working with your child at the beginning of the year or over the summer, before the school year begins. By starting earlier, you give yourself and your child more time to prepare and decrease the pressure as the testing date gets closer.

Summer Vacation

As the school year comes to an end, your child is probably dreaming of warm weather, swimming pools, and sleeping in late. Math, reading, and studying are typically the last things on children's minds.

For many kids, all that sleeping in and hanging out with friends causes them to forget what they learned the year before and does nothing to prepare them for the upcoming school year. Summer vacation is great, but many studies have shown that children forget a lot of what was learned during the school year while they are relaxing over the summer.

Yes, children should enjoy their summer vacation, but there are a few activities they can work on to help them prepare for the next year and help them not be lazy over the summer.

- Have your child attend a summer camp
- Enroll your child in a summer reading program
- Practice on educational websites
- Read some books and write book reports
- Volunteer
- Do chores
- Get a summer job

Remember, a lazy child may become a lazy adult. Make sure your child is active and busy doing something productive.

A child educated only at school is an uneducated child.

~ George Santayana

Reflection and Planning

Grade yourself below:

Code of Conduct	A	B	C
Student Behavior	A	B	C
Emergency Contact	A	B	C
State Testing	A	B	C
Summer Vacation	A	B	C

What are you doing that is great in these areas?

_____

_____

_____

What areas need improvement?

_____

_____

_____

What additional help or information do you need?

_____

_____

_____

New Parent Action Plan for Your Child's Road to Success:

_____

_____

_____

Epilogue

Thank you for taking the time to read how you can help your child. The purpose of this book is to help you, as a parent, to realize that you are a major player in your child's success at school and to provide steps you can take to work with your child at school and at home.

Your child's education is important. Taking the time to get involved may help improve your child's grades and self-esteem, develop hidden talents, and really show your child that you care.

Being an involved parent also allows you to model good parenting for your children so that they will be involved parents for your grandchildren in the future.

Remember, a teacher's job is to plant and water the seeds of education. The parent's job is to make sure the soil is fertile. Your child's education is a hands-on job.

I hope you enjoyed the book and learned some new information. Good luck to you in your educational parenting journey.

Additional Resources

Parenting Websites

www.education.com

www.kidshealth.org

Educational Websites

www.khanacademy.com

www.nationalgeographic.com

www.pbs.org

www.pbskids.org

www.interactivesites.weebly.com

www.funbrain.com

www.collegeboard.com

www.dositey.com

www.alline.org/euro/ereading.html

www.math.com

www.edhelper.com

www.jumpstart.com

www.studyisland.com

Bullying

www.stopbullying.gov

Special Education

www.napcse.org

www.ncld.org

U. S. Department of Education
www.ed.gov

Common Core Educational Standards
www.corestandards.org

Texas Department of Education
www.tea.state.tx.us

School Programs
www.makeawaynow.com

Make A Way is a high relevancy Social Emotional, College and Career Readiness Educational program that empowers at-risk youth and traditionally under served populations.

Curriculum available under the **Make A Way** program include:
Bored of Education
Keep It Moving
10 Things Every Leader MUST Know
Everything You Need to Know Before You Graduate

Suggested Reading
The 7 Habits of Highly Effective People collection
The 5 Love Languages collection
Love and Logic collection

Parent Commitment Agreement

I, _____, parent of _____,
am committed to:

• Make sure my child eats breakfast before school, arrives on time, and has all necessary school supplies daily.

• Make sure my child gets a good night's rest.

• Read the school code of conduct and ensure that my child follows the rules to the best of my ability.

• Praise and encourage my child regularly.

• Frequently monitor my child's grades.

• Attend school functions.

• Make sure my child receives additional academic and/or behavioral assistance as needed.

• Visit my child's classroom at least once a year.

• Find opportunities to volunteer my time and talents.

• Conduct myself respectfully and responsibly when I visit my child's school.

_____   _____
Signature   Date

At the end of the day, the most overwhelming key to a child's success is the positive involvement of parents.

~Jane D. Hull

About the Author

Keysha Chester currently resides in Texas and is a proud wife, mother, and U.S. Navy veteran. She was awarded her Bachelor of Arts in Spanish from the University of Central Florida, her Master's in Education Administration from Lamar University in Texas, and was named 2011-2012 Campus Teacher of the Year..

She knows her job as a parent is very important. She has visited her children's schools, attended parent teacher conferences, volunteered, and is an advocate for her children. She believes that parents should inspect what they expect. Parents expect schools to provide children with a quality education. As a result, parents need to make sure they verify that the schools are doing their job and help by offering support at home.

As a middle school teacher, Keysha has worked on the Site Based Decision Making Committee and the Campus Improvement Team. Her passion is in the area of parental involvement and she has made several recommendations that have been adopted by her campus. She knows the schools really want parents to partner with them by helping at home and having a presence in the schools. Schools know that parental involvement makes a big difference in the life of a child.

Based on the above, Keysha Chester knows both sides of the educational fence. Her book is written based on her life experiences as a parent and an educator. She truly believes that schools and homes should be working together to ensure that all children receive a quality education.

To contact or book
Keysha Chester for:

Parenting Seminars
School Staff Developments
Parenting with Love and Logic
Family and Life Coaching
9 Essential Skills for the Love and Logic Classroom

404-597-4645

ktchester1@gmail.com

Notes

Notes

Notes